The Red and Yellow Book

Kelvin Corcoran

Shearsman Library

Second Edition.
Published in the United Kingdom in 2019 by
Shearsman Library
an imprint of Shearsman Books
by Shearsman Books Ltd
50 Westons Hill Drive
Emersons Green
BRISTOL
BS16 7DF

Shearsman Books Ltd Registered Office
30–31 St. James Place, Mangotsfield, Bristol BS16 9JB
(this address not for correspondence)

www.shearsman.com

ISBN 978-1-84861-634-9

First published by Textures, Southsea, 1986.

Not that voice

the trees and grass come up for air
a man shouts through the crowd, I could
with the blackberries of that sun
but the faces wobble my head in your lap

in this other city; its little lakes and frigid ducks,
Dantes is a removal firm, the man is not a rhetorical figure
shouting at the scene of the murder, an underwater duck
is a plastic carrier full of water that surrounds it

give me that burger, that friend
I never want to leave, I mean to save your life
check trousers comma did she
touch with hands like mine

catachresis, Alabama and its moon
dark when you go, dark the bed when you come
O moon, O mad sex against the city of business men
hold hard in the lodge of our aging

Power Lust and Striving

all evidence is taped, these rats have bubonic plague
would you challenge the fleet, silver grey it sparkles
bobbing off-shore I have been home all day
the ports are blocked with French farmers twenty deep

this is meat, this is your photograph
the food is fat in Panama, you sang
my own fire, my own true fire
in the exchange there is a secret message

regresses nervously along the circuit fibre of the forgotten tomb,
it is 6.30 already and gale force winds toboggan
this secret shit, did I do that and did you?
there is a golden chain of love

all day the weather rocked the house
boomed about and called February
the bomb of Spring is ticking,
the people of China do not starve

Keep

the town was tourist wrapped and ticking
the sun shone through they only dream of me,
despite going down on Wall Street
sleep and sleep for England

guilts eased but with doll figures
bigger than expected sugar and lemon granules
lift and drink as easy as selling sweets to kids,
with the engine of my performance
a clean bra and knickers in case I fall

they call women girls but only dream of me,
buttocky stable lads beam in the pre-dawn
they are handsome men in Cotswold summer
sleep and money and my steady voice
sleep and sleep for England

there's a wedding and I'm waiting
with the red and yellow book,
it's big and bright
each poem a maze
the words in relief,
somebody reads and we eat, drink and dance
I check what poems to read –
the hot symbolism of dawn rolls out
green and lush the air falls
over my head and onto my hands
the world pops up a 3D book,
I remember what was happening
in the sun, attendant warmth
rising to meet it
a fat man puts his foot on the book
which can take it, it's strong
can slay its enemies
but I rescue it all the same,
the food is cleared off tables
and there's hectic dancing
now?   as all this happens
      I am fixed on my book
      which is bright and can take it

she smashed the glass and swept it up,
at home a husband of 56 year old baby fat
followed me through my life
Spring rips through the world, everything looks good
this is the fifth line, made it o.k.

– it was a petrol glass

you breathe out, I hear cooking
imagine rich people with emotional problems
it's heaven, it's probably Paul Newman
and certain domestic appliances hummed on,
I think he can deal with it

paintings in hospitals can help;
local scenes, the haywain, a good frame
or the two cartoonish kids looking at the moon,
they are folksy and sit on a bench
they are rumpled and happy

– I am not joking

For a long time when reading books of philosophy I mistook
casual for causal. Philosophy seemed more entertaining
than it turned out to be and imagine how loose-limbed the
world became, even without examples.

Say twenty cubes, on each face of each cube part of one of the
six jigsaw pictures. The feel of them is good, their size, the wood
and six pictures plus hybrids. No matter how casual you are they
fit together so well, edge to edge, the wood, with a nice knock, they
always fit.

Despite the feebleness of this conceit, for a long time when reading
– what do you expect?

But still part of Ivor the Engine patrols the sea
below a girl's nose and mouth joins the snowy mountains
to something uncertain which hovers above
the Indian camp of musical instruments
torpedoing a partial jungle of just red.

Of all that Nature doth entend

He is a great magician
and handsome, everyday
I wear the clothes but
to see those you love
in the knowledge of general terms,
get your foot off mine
with explosives you can
I mean him, gold gold
in this film a bullet is an explosion of paint,
John/Juan mouth to mouth
accelerated the lines of consumption
indicate out and drop a gear
push it foot and hand.
Afraid to use the unwritten words,
bandito discovered, lost since birth
the fly buzz, never known before
go faster and that man is in trouble
what kind? Picture in the paper kind.
The what just grows up
through your body like satyriasis
in a field of hairy balls
make European foodstuffs.
Pick the tune I don't know
the inaccessible music of feeling

in a hand-held world
it all goes word bang, that sadness
deep eye in head of horse
ghost train in false glasses
and there is only power,
on the trams, in the yards
talked seriously, said comrade
my/his hands shake
outside the bank of all that money
all that serge underwear
and iniquitous economics,
that face too close.
I like to look, with my fingers
no part of your body
far from another
flute music never tasted so sweet

– I wanted to take her in my arms,
she sleeps it down over the bridge
which crosses a dry river
aim your gun, answer me
heaven comes in a myth of light
of diamorphine
I hope
against all men who know.

the last poem

– no death is an average death

I wish I could get my voice back oh

the fields where you grew are burning

– would you like your bed jacket now?
Yes   I   think   I   will

fear no more the heat of

the last word – drink –

8.50 p.m. 9 August 1984

– we're with you mum (kiss)

in my arms, all gone
a Mannerist portrait
58 years old, all gone

Next

hardest of all thins to morning
down the petrolled ways,
see the girl ride her bike along the path
safer that way, I check the tyres,
I float in a clean shaven sky
no more to talk and hold your hand
palm against palm for the dying months,
the first person a fiction now

the dead do not talk
we are not with them

one
breath
another
the dark roof
rests
on the white walls

this is Radio Wittgenstein calling
possessed of invisible splendour
and a sunny morning wind in the roses
is all the case is in a carpeted fold
safe from the living air
and the flaming circle of our days

they really use this language
they mean to do these things,
show me your leg, how it feels inside
smooth as a wedding ring, fast as a travel show
where we go fallible and unfixed

I follow the argument of this book
between machine days
and all that I can't believe,
the little door opens
a smell of resin and 3 o'clock dark,
the faces rush to the sides

the soil of the garden is damp
the apples come into taste and
kids in the street play guess the tv show,
there is traffic or there isn't
there is nothing in the paper,
just faces, just writing

my sister said

it's like my body twisting round
crying in me, twisting me round
when it rains, I think of her
           in all that mud

By the window in an easy chair
spectral grey and thin as light
her eyes fixed alive on her grandchildren.

*

The newly dead look dead so soon,
her black black hair
over the gone face,
not my mother then.

*

Two steps down

He didn't visit very often
spent time and money
in the pub, a small place
below the level of the pavement.

Monday is pension day,
Thursday spent out, penitential flowers.
'Have you seen dad or anybody?'
'Take two steps down, you'll find him.'

*

Home for the last time, out of the hospital, home because one of us would always be there. She sat in her chair, legs propped, never asleep. All night I listened to her breathing and gave the elixir every four hours. Unable to lie down, pressure sores, legs swollen, lungs filling up.

Eyes calm and holding hands she said – When I had so many kids people said I was stupid, but they're not saying that now. Later, when I wasn't there – Oh he does make a fuss of me.

In the morning we watched Tarzan and then the visitors came.

On hearing the song of the dog

A heaving landscape is ornamented;
Pegasus shrieking leaps from a hill
as cupids dance slapstick in a ring
and two others, impaled against a stormy sky,
drop rigid roses and other equipment.
'I don't mind really, I can understand
why people confuse fiction with reality
but I'm not a bit like Mavis Riley.'

This exchange can exclude all civilian lines,
out across the map of western Europe
the suck of the sand, the literal surf
the diamonds of my waking wash my feet.
We are all in this, we saw films on what to do,
food riots, that sort of stuff.

At night the third and perfect body,
what mind behind those eyes?
Which woman, which man?
The Miro blue of the night
lit from beneath by the street and houses of us
and the dark trees of the hold we have.

We were a high spirited crew aboard the Melusia,
in the dark mountains rivers run
rivers of gold, cool and bright
stuffed with gold and babbling oh my
it makes all the difference.

Some of us do not like princes
nor women paid to sweat it out in furs and leather,
it makes all the difference what you do,
most striking of all are the women of the valley
such noble girls before the white man,
the celebrants at a pig feast
who build schools on asbestos tips.

You are on this island in deep water,
the corporate tricks and reluctant decisions
in the voices of the land that time forgot;
walking about, in the bar, on the air, in the shops
the revolting confidence of ownership,
each turns a page of English history
it fingers you and gets it wrong.

In the angry dark
her house fades;
she sang to herself
she made cakes
in the kitchen
with plants at the window,
the easy talk all gone.

The dead take us with them
but we are not the same,
it's cruel enough
in this darkness
the face that fits my face
gone, my name unmade.

I was with my mother when she died, by the bed in the corner of the ward. Quiet after visiting time, her brother and sister and my sisters. The doctor had said at mid-day, 'It won't be long now, she'll soon be free of it.'

I went up town to buy the ginger beer she wanted, small bottles with screw tops. My final thing for you, and until this last day you held the glass yourself. In the teeth of death a human act.
The day before I'd been called back to the hospital to get rid of my father, drunk and talking about euthanasia. Only the medically qualified understand alcoholics. He left noisily but she was beyond embarrassment then.

I sat on one side holding her hand, her sister on the other. Through six months she was gentle and kind to us all. I could feel no strength in her hot and cold hands.

Her shallow breathing stopped, stopped, in suddenly, taking the chin and lower face as well. Not her face then. I watched the last pulse in her neck, kissed her forehead and said, 'We're with you mum.' Then the Sister said, 'She's gone, she's at peace now.'

I was with my mother when — after so long it seemed hurried.

> A gentle woman of great strength
> she raised five children in love.

The moral climate I had in mind is not
natural. It is the product of a particular
architecture, A fascist band, a slave market
is a community of men – of a sort.

The book had no pictures or conversations in it.
It was of no interest at all, she thought.

Todtnauberg, the Black Forest
8 April 1926
Edmund and Martin.

Here's another card,
one of my favourites,
see you on the 17th
Rothko Black on Maroon.

From each dark corner
and unoccupied house
came the howl of the dogs
unlike words but of the solid night.

Ten water colours made from that star.
It was an engraving after Moorland
except for a hole kicked through the centre.

The sound at the end of waiting

Through the jammed layers of separate intentions
in the city of lead and gold,
solid as carbon and the shining air
with the wipers fused across the slab of day
just no time ashes the shoulder pain
stuck up the councillor's piratised bus route.

Breathe out and think of the word – relax,
under the apparent coral reef
hit and miss music starts all over the place,
factual, certain of itself and anxious;
the brutality of facts in the box of delights
will open bright in your face.

Then it all breaks down like Muybridge,
traffic and trees stuck in grey and white;
the passive geometry isn't a picture
it's there, what the papers say in solid air
one morning imposed on another,
at the next junction the sky condenses.

*

He lived in the forest and thought language life,
he knew crowds of faces that were themselves,
that did not float, but were held in falling everyday.
At the end of five, tired and chopped into segments,
weak in the chest and falling forward
his hands full of the night at the end of the garden.

The that he felt spelt hunger, the forest and
the forest of lights, cars, holidays, faces –
hunger was the imprint, the clearing of Tuesday maybe.
To refine to simple terms meant loss,
you could buy it but the shops were often closed,
only puns rang the till in the towns of the great inflation.

He knew books of pictures and gems of green and red,
they made a story which lit up his face;
a secret aquarium, a secret forest in hand-held words.
Imagine the whole field by any light,
each day glimmers in miniature on the calendar
a series of Palmer landscapes flick over and fit one on the other.

Stray conversations, chairs he sat in and string,
the empty never empty of itself – but string?
Disgusting in this bar, so much like the wreck of the anthill.

Work on the Rhine dykes taught him nothing,
just mud, just cement of a new order of feeling
as the pincers of Russia and America close in.

The sky was vast and blue with a do-what-you-will consistency,
along the road you expect the sea, choppy, fresh and populated,
but the authentic man has clean hands and is resolved,
a barbarian with a pure dialect
— it makes all the difference what you do.

        This has gone wrong, what escapes
        the sun or dry wall of coveted rooms
        and the commerce up town, I don't know.
        Digging the heat from the rolling sea
        or cold fronts clipping across our sky space,
        how can I get him for what he said?
        Although it's January I'm warm
        and joining the dots; it's Economics,
        the current repressive intelligence
        or a runaway train full of children
        or duck and ducklings fat on the pond.
        Each day transparent, tangible and involved
        we walk abroad on the air supported
        and it's bin liners and Ready Brek I want,

the politics of more than one country
the many lives tied at your hand.
Walk in this impossible knowledge
but definite as the printed word,
the body as starting point in the philosophy of flesh.

Across the way in the dark there are boundaries,
polished paving stones laid along the path,
horizon of moon, streetlights, trees and houses
lit from below, it's not hylozoic, it's ours;
we walk to the late open off-licence
and you blonde every monochrome street of new year's eve.

*

The shapes and colours of the green world
wrapped in the town map on warm, middle tint paper
as the crowds of Saturday heightened with body colour
people a golden and mirrored shopping arcade.
Hi, my name's Tracey, I'm a student of phenomenology.
Telescoped arches belly up to ultramarine skies.
We need to see the five days it cost,
we need to see human obligations.

Hi, I'm Tracey the shapes and colours of the green world,
sepia mixed with gum then glazed, flaked off and didn't last.
You don't look at people's faces closely enough.

*

Above the garages the January moon rises,
guess how old he was when he wrote
Ode to Michael Goldberg ('s Birth and other Births)?
It's cold out there but I'm warm in here,
the east coast under snow and intensified policing
ice snakes up the roads across the country.
We the common people have ancestors and blood,
moon smack in my face launches into snowy clouds
as 27 years ago Frank in winter early spring.

I pull back the curtain, the crust on my head cracks,
the metallic light of morning and night coming
picks up the tarmac and ascending windows;
a lovely blue like a freezer flaking off an aria sky.
We have blood and I have you on the carpet
I shall enter in under that arch
more gentle than July before an early death
or, as if, in the very heart of loss

the steady voice of Alec Guinness says,
'. . . on the very next day', what you want to hear
and were about to say.

That voice remains like a dream when you wake
as the mayor of your home town in the shining day,
where your family and friends are alive again
in the first house of a perfect childhood;
the red and blue triangular sails of the yachts
slip down the river of familiar afternoons
between seemingly fields of sprouts and chrysanthemums,
and on the far side a reasonably shaped hill
holds a railway line for black and green locomotives.

I stared from the back-step, it was exactly like this;
she piled up the ironing, sang to herself,
looked at me and care was in the world.
I dreamt of a rowing boat that rocked me skyward,
I didn't want to float into that anaesthesia,
bring me back out of thin air,
spread straight from the knife it ends the story.

*

Snow falling in pop songs dumb dumb,
what do I do tomorrow whilst little shapes
falling skid a rubber car down canals
with horrible echoes all over the rock,
two lines of traffic brake, cannot hold that shape,
how do tomorrow when others jigsaw talk,
his teeth in your mouth
snow falling on the whole world, crepuscular and infected,
the light wheel flutters in my hands,
this is it – with no control you carry on.
If that's the case I'm leaving.

Double pearl, fire and ruby bear her name,
how did it start snow falling?
Mountainous sky of non-verbal weather
experienced antibiotics in nervous tracks,
across the sky opens snow and out falls
a complete town, the powder of light, the many lives.

Why don't you lift the piano lid to play that tune?
It's not a piano, it's a poor metaphor,
see my fingers presentive,
presentive fingers playing a metaphor

like polar bears dive from glaciers to fish
or my foot arch curls with secret warmth;
the final continent beyond analogy
here are the poor, they have number,
the adults with worn hands of too much care.

The sky hits your head, it's so cold
a door slams in your chest,
shock settles like breath in the garden,
chestnut leaves falling on the grave of Martin Heidegger.
That wave held be careful how you drive
foam engineering, a lorry takes a corner
a string of red lights comes on
against the iron hills age
ancient Europe, those people up there
that face looking out for me.

from The Red and Yellow Book

The house fronts flip over
subterranean rivers surface in
public fountains of gods and tortured horses,
brown and rabid near the rapist's carpark
the grand sweep of the municipal offices,
see the hand moving, its trick
the truth has made us free.

*

Clouds pile up in the sky
anvil   lemon   cicatrix
with the industrial revolution
marriage, divorce and public health.
William, it was English poetry too,
in the circle of our blood
blinking like moles through the other side of winter,
in the fields of Peterloo
in the valley thick with corn
the kind man reads a world revealed.
Honey flows in the sky
piles of soap and hot bread
in the streets smell the earth,
bright buds clean as bullets

the polished cars and public lies,
they are what they do.

*

To find the western path
I breakfasted swords big sun
                    gates of and
at first breath   bird song
happy in the stupid heart,
the fool with his finger on the trigger
no further forward for men and women,
hot days of rubbish letters
surface to surface arrows
telekinesis and country music
spark across the imperial world.

*

Rain on April streets and cars,
the occupation forces hold the populists' gazebo;
no sweet moderation shines in Port Albion.
Walls of sound of sea made them soft and witless;

hamsters in perspex balls
daffodils and socket sets
markets crash and banks roar,
they dream wealth creation in elected bodies
and we all fall down.

*

Another life in a sparrow's wing
spreads above the prisoners,
running through the desert
they leave coils of rope and clouds of red dust;
having modified their experience
the look of the sentence and the title
emanated a spell – shazam –
the bristling globe, the shores of men and women
silk descending folds around
the piano keys nervous itch
as Jackson Pollack trees scratch the sky
balloons absorb each other, the green garages
and unknown pedestrians in an opera of no pain.

*

Just look, In-der-Welt-sein
but nowhere to park the car,
it rains local newspaper lies
about a town nobody lives in,
it means a fistful of mush or
darkness in the kitchen on tottering legs.
In seed time learn the beautiful history,
I must wash my hair
I must be happy
                    the first dictionary
had only four words
I will tell you what they are,
you will live a better life.

*

Open your hands, let them go
there's no going back to that world,
this room has many pictures
I think of the beginning book
silver tried in a furnace of earth
up to the elbows shines in words,
before meanings the restraint is all
as Spring rattles its couplings

birds fornicate in bare trees
the light flicks a switch in their eyes
fuses blowing everywhere,
the dark earth and its smell
grows onyx, carnelian, quartz
the fifth and greatest monarchy;
I know you in my hands
the level streets of a life before us.

*

Day into day, night into night speaks
far off and exceeding deep
in all the houses that are lived in
broad sunlight through the park.
I buy a pineapple at the Chinese grocers
warm that house, it's Greek to you,
a woman is wearing pink trousers
she walks in morning and legs
opens shop doors, the happy actors on blocks
write sky on a banner above the street,
they pretend everything is O.K.
a street in the sky, the real sky
in blue capitals the language of delivery.

*

Around all all
the need to say
what it is to wake with you
not one touch
can I say
or measure
you naked
seem just from the sun
always and
waking find you
hold delight
a shape inside
each other
we walk in
day to day
not one word
can speak the lustre
of that touch
I breathe you
the dumb speak
the secret body
of one life
leaving only
a verbal substance
on our fingers.